This journal belongs to:

Published by Sourcebooks
P.O. Box 4410, Naperville, Illinois 60567-4410
(630) 961-3900
sourcebooks.com

Printed and bound in the United States of America.
VP 10 9 8 7 6 5 4 3 2 1

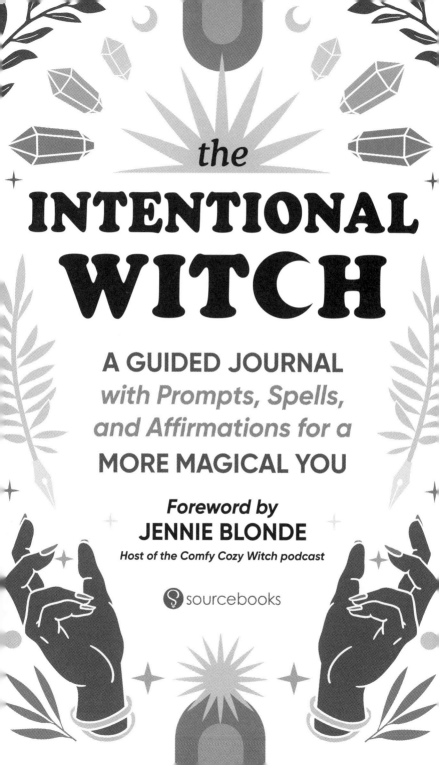

the
INTENTIONAL
WITCH

A GUIDED JOURNAL
with Prompts, Spells, and Affirmations for a
MORE MAGICAL YOU

Foreword by
JENNIE BLONDE
Host of the Comfy Cozy Witch podcast

sourcebooks

Foreword

When I was first asked to write the foreword to a book about intentional witchcraft, my answer was immediately an enthusiastic yes! Bridging together two of my passions—witchcraft and journaling—*The Intentional Witch: A Guided Journal* encapsulates all the comfort and coziness I love in a magical practice, and brings together two things I find vital. I need magic in my everyday practice to be meaningful and intentional in nature, and I also need space to reflect on my spiritual journey. I've been journaling about my practice for years and love to look back through my old Books of Shadows and grimoires to see how much I've changed and how far I've come, and to reminisce about the beginnings of my magic when I had no clue what I was doing. Reflection is such an important part of my practice, and something I do on a daily basis and urge others to do as well.

It's no surprise to those who know me or who listen to my podcast that I am a firm believer in finding magic in the small things, in the everyday, and I'm always searching for small meaningful ways to do just that. Since starting my *Comfy Cozy Witch* podcast, a question I get over and over again is "Where do I even begin?" Many feel pressured and overwhelmed by all the information, oftentimes conflicting information, about the craft. Although I tell most listeners to begin by listening to episodes of the podcast for inspiration or to visit their local spiritual shops, I'm always looking for book resources to recommend that urge new practitioners to start small. The guided journal in your hands is a resource I stand behind that does just that. Not only does it give solid beginner witch information like meanings of herbs, an overview of crystals, the significance of each candle color, and more; it also serves as a book to help you put intention into action through a variety of journal prompts and daily affirmations, all while allowing you to reflect on your spiritual journey. I also love how this guided journal helps connect you to magic through small meaningful rituals, thought-provoking magical prompts, and affirming mantras.

Whether you're just starting out on your spiritual journey, curious about how to live life with more intention and direction, or looking for a way to reconnect to yourself and to your magical practice, *The Intentional Witch: A Guided Journal* truly has something for everyone. Not to mention, it makes this comfy cozy witch feel just like her name—comfy, cozy, and witchy.

Enjoy, my magical friends!

Bright blessings,

Jennie Blonde

Color!

The Intentional Witch

It's hard to be a witch in this fast-paced world. While you are at work and running errands, spells are forgotten and herbs dry up. When you barely have time to charge your phone, charging your crystals is hardly a priority. And why does your roommate think all your witching supplies are trash?

This is a journal to help you get back on track. *The Intentional Witch* is for the spellcaster who wants to tap into their magic energy. Whether you are returning to witchcraft or just starting, this journal has over one hundred and fifty prompts, activities, and exercises to help you ground yourself, grow your magical talents, and blossom into the goddess you were meant to be. This journal was concocted with a mixture of affirmations, self-affirming activities, and magic spells. Feel free to work through it at your own pace.

Don't forget to keep track of your spells in the back of this journal.

Dust off your crystals, and find that broom. Now is when you manifest your powers!

Witch's Tool Kit

Every witch needs supplies. Each person has an energy and will react differently to different materials. You may need to try multiple versions of an item before finding one that works. Here is a baseline list of materials you may want to use as you complete this journal. Feel free to scavenge items or buy new, and expand or edit the list as you like. Intention matters more than the item itself.

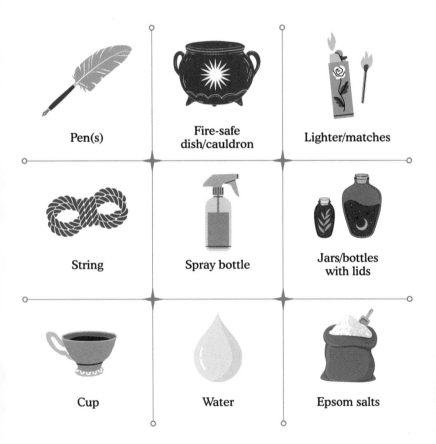

Pen(s)	Fire-safe dish/cauldron	Lighter/matches
String	Spray bottle	Jars/bottles with lids
Cup	Water	Epsom salts

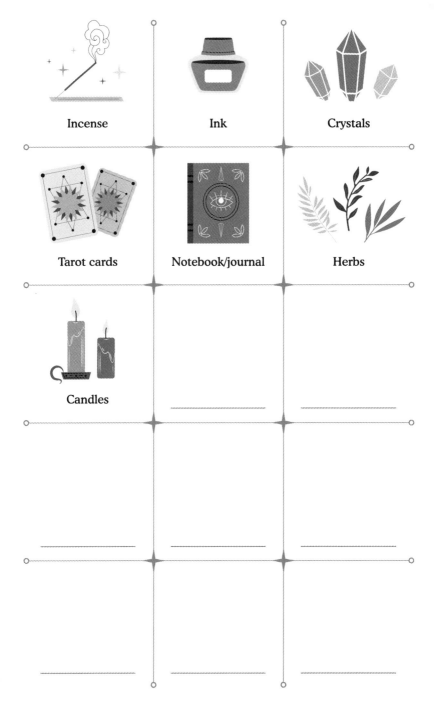

Incense

Ink

Crystals

Tarot cards

Notebook/journal

Herbs

Candles

A Guide to Candles

Every witch needs candles. Candles are great for performing or enhancing spells. Each color has associated meanings and properties. White candles have the added use of being capable substitutes if you don't have other colors on hand. Several spells and activities include candles of various colors. Think about which ones you might need and how you might combine them to best suit your intention!

My Candles

COLOR	POWERS AND PROPERTIES	WAX FROM YOUR CANDLE
Red	attraction between human souls	
Orange	creation and adventure	
Yellow	consideration and growth	
Green	healing and prosperity	
Light Blue	truth and acceptance	
Dark Blue	intuition and perception	
Purple	wisdom and enlightenment	
Pink	romance, specifically emotional connection, and self-care	
Brown	grounding and stability	
Black	amplifying magical strength (use sparingly)	
White	peace (can be used in lieu of other colors)	

An Introduction to Crystals

Every witch needs crystals. Like candles, crystals and other charged stones are great for performing or enhancing spells, or inviting certain energy into your life. Crystals and stones each have their own properties, and some are associated with particular months. Several spells and activities include various crystals. Clear quartz can be used as a substitute for any crystal. Take stock of your current crystal inventory, and decide whether you want to add to your collection.

My Crystals

STONE	PROPERTIES	MONTHLY ASSOCIATION	STOCK
Clear Quartz	spiritual connection	January	
Rose Quartz	balance between heavens and earth	February	
Aventurine	balance and luck	March	
Carnelian	physical desires	April	
Amber	warmth and recovery	May	

STONE	PROPERTIES	MONTHLY ASSOCIATION	STOCK
Citrine	clear-mindedness	June	
Lapis	clear communication	July	
Red Tiger's Eye	grounding and protection	August	
Fluorite	order and focus	September	
Dark Amethyst	understanding and intuition	October	
Light Amethyst	spiritual awareness	October	
Labradorite	enhances psychic abilities	November	
Garnet	willpower and courage	December	
Jade	money and love	N/A	
Kunzite	power and good luck	N/A	
Orange Calcite	creativity	N/A	
Sodalite	speaking openly	N/A	
Topaz	self-realization and confidence	N/A	

A Field Guide to Herbs

Every witch needs herbs. Herbs are also essential for performing or enhancing spells, and can even be incorporated into meals. Herbs have their own properties to be mindful of when following along with the spells and activities in this journal. Rosemary is a great substitute if you do not have a particular herb. Take note of the ones you do have or want to acquire, live plants and dried.

My Herbs

HERBS	PROPERTIES	STOCK
Basil	blessings	
Bay Leaf	wisdom and vision	
Catnip	relaxation and attracting love	
Chamomile	tranquility and harmony	
Cinnamon	passion and shielding	
Dandelion	wishes and luck	
Lavender	purification and sleep	
Lemon Peel	cleansing	
Mint	luck and attracting money	
Mugwort	enhances psychic abilities	
Orange Peel	luck and joy	
Pine	moderation and prosperity	
Rose	love and beauty	
Rosemary	vitality and purification	
Sage	home blessing and cleansing	
Thyme	beauty and courage	

I am that witch!

Start your magical journey fresh with a new spell book to track your witchy accomplishments and write down all your spells.

I declare my intentions.

What goals are you striving towards this year? Write them on these pages to manifest.

I am
aligned
with
the
Earth.

A white candle is the perfect instrument to represent all the elements. Earth is represented in the candle itself. Air is represented by the smoke from the flame. Water is represented in the melted wax. Fire is represented in the flame itself.

My words have power.

Light a white candle while chanting a spell or manifestation that resonates with you at this moment. If you don't have a white candle, any candle will work in a pinch, but visualize a white light while chanting. Repetition is often the key to successful manifestation.

My positive attitude is its own protection.

Clear quartz has powerful protective properties and can be a stand-in for any other crystal. Select a clear quartz for your witch use, or find a shiny pebble to stand in for it.

I have the power to enhance my own environment.

Write about your search for clear quartz here, and refer to this entry to help you find future crystals.

How can you incorporate your clear quartz into your daily witch practices?

_____

_____

_____

_____

_____

_____

_____

_____

_____

_____

_____

_____

_____

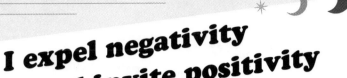

I expel negativity and invite positivity into my life.

List the things in your life that have negative energy and are no longer serving you. After that, cross out the items to metaphorically remove them from your life.

_____

_____

_____

_____

_____

_____

_____

_____

_____

_____

_____

_____

_____

_____

_____

I allow
my magic
to guide me
to compassion.

Clear quartz is perfect for clearing any excess negativity; keep one
with you and use it to facilitate a spell of compassion around you.
No quartz? Focus your energy with periodic pauses by closing your
eyes and removing any energy that isn't serving you.

I am ready
to begin again.

Cleansing Potion					IDEAL TIME TO CAST
					when required

	STONES	HERBS	CANDLES	SIGILS	OBJECTS	OTHER
INGREDIENTS	rose quartz	rosemary sprig	none	none	spray bottle	moonlight-infused water

WORDS

a manifestation of your choice that invites positive energy and casts out negative energy

INSTRUCTIONS

To banish negative energy from your life, cast the following spell:

1. Fill spray bottle halfway with water.

2. Leave bottle on windowsill overnight on a full moon to infuse.

3. Add a rosemary sprig and rose quartz to bottle.

4. Seal and spray the potion in spaces with negative energy to cleanse and attract positive feelings.

Spell Record

DATE	TIME	SEASON	MOON	RESULT
			◯	
			◯	
			◯	
			◯	
			◯	
			◯	
			◯	
			◯	
			◯	

I allow the essence of love to wash over me.

Enjoy a rose-scented self-care ritual by placing dried or fresh rose petals in a large bowl, pouring hot water over them, and letting the steam bathe your face in the magical essence of roses.

Write about your experience here, noting the sensations you experienced.

I enjoy discovering the love in my life.

Use this space to write down what love means to you. How do you see love manifest in your life (romantic, platonic, self-love)?

This will create an excellent reference for any love spells you cast in the future.

_____

_____

_____

_____

_____

_____

_____

_____

_____

_____

_____

_____

_____

I bring good energy with me wherever I go.

Stir your morning beverage clockwise three times while saying, "I stir in good energy." Sip good energy into your day while you enjoy your beverage. What did you notice?

I send love into the universe.

Pink candles bring love and positivity to any ritual and are particu-
larly useful in spell work for friendship, relaxation, and acceptance.
White candles can be used as an alternative for any color candle
while you visualize the color you wish to work with or incorporate
it into the spell work with another item you have handy, such as a
scarf, thread, or art.

Write about the positive relationships you have in your life.
Who lifts you up? Why are you grateful for them?

My world is full of love.

Rose quartz is a wonderful crystal for amplifying joy, bringing in love, and promoting a sense of peace. Select a rose quartz or find a natural alternative (any item that gives you feelings of love) to represent it in your spell work. Write down a few love spells here to refer to as needed. You can write several, focusing on different types of love, including self-love, romantic love, and platonic love.

_____

_____

_____

_____

_____

_____

_____

_____

_____

_____

_____

I connect with the love that lives inside of me.

Using a needle or toothpick, carve the first letter of your name into a pink candle. While you light it, chant one of your love spells.

Write your spell down a few times on this page to help bring it to life.

_____

_____

_____

_____

_____

_____

_____

_____

_____

_____

_____

_____

I accept that I cannot change everything.

Pink candles are a powerful tool for acceptance.

Write down something you are having a hard time accepting and place it under a dish containing a pink candle. Use the power of the flame to burn away some of your lingering struggles.

I accept that I have the agency and autonomy to change what I can.

What are some ways you can create tangible change in your life now? Include some strategies for how to do so.

I spread love everywhere.

Place small pieces of rose quartz in a spray bottle and add water to create a room spray infused with the positive energies of rose quartz.

Write about any changes you notice as a result.

Abundance is drawn to me.

Place rose petals somewhere that you would like to attract abundance. Ideas could include in your fridge to bring an abundance of food, on your altar to bring an abundance of magic, or under your television to bring an abundance of excellent things to watch.

Where would you like to find more abundance in your life? How can you make it happen?

I grant myself grace.

Holding a rose quartz in your hands, charge it with self-compassion, and carry it with you as a reminder that you can grant yourself grace. How can you give yourself more grace and compassion?

I release myself from negative self-talk.

Your mind is your own, just as your body is. Challenge any negative thoughts that come to mind. What are they rooted in? Are they true? Redirect negative thoughts to something more positive or neutral. Reflect on your experiences here.

My fresh mindset attracts what is best for me.

Mint is a fabulously easy-to-grow herb that is used in a variety of spell work focused on luck, travel, and protection. Pin a sprig near you as you work, and let the fresh ideas flow.

I deserve the best of what the universe has to offer.

Aromatherapy is a wonderful sensory experience. Immerse yourself in your favorite scents. What do you notice as your chosen scent fills your space? Write about any physical sensations or thoughts that come to mind.

_____

_____

_____

_____

_____

_____

_____

_____

_____

_____

_____

My magic is stronger every day.

While holding a piece of aventurine in your hand, charge it with success. Carry it with you as needed. No aventurine? Write down your goals here, and then choose one to hold on to, in your mind or literally in your pocket. Manifest through your continued focus.

I allow my magic to guide me to growth.

Write down one word that embodies what you hope to grow and bury it in the ground outside your home to let the Earth aid in your manifestation.

I am part of the Earth.

Ground yourself by going on a walk. Enhance your walk with mindfulness, paying close attention to the five senses as you go. Write down what you saw, heard, smelled, felt, and tasted on your walk.

_____

_____

_____

_____

_____

_____

_____

_____

_____

_____

_____

_____

_____

_____

I am in harmony with the Earth.

Green candles embody the energy of the Earth and are wonderful for prosperity, growth, and success magic. Invite the energy of the Earth into your every day by burning a green candle or using a white candle that you have visualized green energy over. Write down some Earth-inspired manifestations here.

I speak the language of the universe.

Mint is a powerful tool for enhancing communication. Make a cup of mint tea to add its strength to your voice. While it steeps, breathe in the aroma and visualize finding the best words to manifest your goals. Write down the goals you want to focus on here.

I bring myself financial security.

Create a money-attracting spell by carving slots all over a green candle and placing dimes inside them. Write your spell here. Light the candle and listen to the dimes fall as you visualize the money coming to you while the candle burns.

I take charge of my own life.

Sigils are powerful tools to engage with in your magical practice. They are visual representations of a witch's desired outcome from spell work.

Destructible sigils are activated once they are destroyed because the energy is found in the act of destroying it, usually through fire, water, or other substances.

Temporary sigils are intended to last for a short while and are well suited for intentions you feel you need to focus on longer. Temporary sigils are usually drawn on the skin, candles, or anywhere the sigil will dissipate naturally.

Permanent sigils are made to last forever—or at least for a very long time. Permanent sigils are often created through artwork such as a painting or pottery, or carved into a piece of furniture you intend to keep for a long while.

I speak, and the universe answers.

Write down some intentions you want to manifest into reality through the use of a sigil.

_____

_____

_____

_____

_____

_____

_____

_____

_____

_____

_____

_____

_____

I create my reality.

Draw a simple sigil based on one of your intentions from the previous page, the more specific, the better.

Begin by writing a sentence in the present tense defining your intent such as, "I am free of stress and anxiety." Remove all the vowels and repeated letters in your sentence. Design your sigil from the remaining letters on the following page.

Once you are satisfied with your sigil, remove the page from this journal and burn it in a fire-safe container.

You may want to explore temporary and permanent sigils as well, depending on your current goals and intentions.

Draw your sigil!

I embrace renewal.

Light a green candle, and let it burn while you do light stretches. This candle honors and supports your capacity for revitalization and renewal.

How do you engage in restful and rejuvenating practices?

_____

_____

_____

_____

_____

_____

_____

_____

_____

_____

_____

_____

Nature is a part of me.

Plant mint seeds in a small pot to keep in the kitchen year-round, or plant outside when the weather allows. If time doesn't allow you to plant them yourself, many nurseries have them already beautifully potted.

Working with the literal earth is a wonderful way to honor the world you live in. How can you bring the Earth into your daily life?

I love myself, nature, and my magic.

Spending time outside is a wonderful way to connect with the energies of the Earth. Note the changing landscape as spring progresses and how that symbolism overlaps with your practice.

Write about one of your mindful experiences outside here.

I believe in
my own magic.

Confidence is key when making magic work for you. Make a list of three things you do that bring you confidence, and try to enact all three today.

I embrace new opportunities with confidence.

Red candles are used for confidence, passion, and determination. These qualities make red candles excellent for new beginnings.

Pick an area of intention to focus, on and write a few manifestations here. Light a red candle while speaking them aloud.

_____

_____

_____

_____

_____

_____

_____

_____

_____

_____

_____

_____

I will greet today with fiery enthusiasm.

Carnelians embody fire and as such are amazing crystals for work with vitality, protection, and focus. Find a carnelian or an alternative that fills you with fiery energy.

Write about what made you select this for your current magical work.

I use the tools available to me to get the results I want.

Red ink adds power, strength, and confidence to your written spells.

Write out a spell (or three!) here in red ink, and speak them out loud to lock them in.

_____

_____

_____

_____

_____

_____

_____

_____

_____

_____

_____

_____

_____

Caring for the environment is caring for myself.

Self-care is also taking care of the environment that we live in. Upcycle old glass jars for spell work by removing the labels and thoroughly cleaning them with dish soap.

Brainstorm ideas for spells you'd like to perform with spell jars here.

I am full of happiness for the future.

Catnip is an herb best known because of our feline friends, but it is also a strong magical herb used in spell work for friendship, happiness, and courage. Take time today to meditate on what those words mean to you and how you can use that knowledge in your future spell work.

I am worthy of admiration.

Celebrate your self-confidence by creating a dedication to yourself with your favorite pictures, awards, and mementos of your favorite times. Write your dedication here, or make a physical shrine to remind yourself of all you have accomplished.

Allow this to be part of the light that guides you to accomplishing your goals.

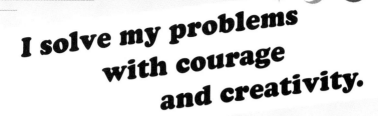

I solve my problems with courage and creativity.

Think about a bad day you had recently. What happened that was good that day? What can you do to keep the same problems from happening again?

For a boost to your vitality (and creativity!), wear a carnelian as a necklace or place one in your pocket. Lean on this energy to help support you today.

_____

_____

_____

_____

_____

_____

_____

_____

_____

_____

I bring the power of fire to all that I do.

A cauldron not only looks super witchy, but it is also a great tool for safe work with flame and fire. Smoke-cleanse your cauldron to prepare it for your magical workings by burning any combination of herbs or incense inside it. Any fire-safe dish makes for a great cauldron.

What are some spells you can perform with your cauldron?

(Tip: think of spells and items that are enhanced by fire!)

I am aware of my magic, and I share it with the world.

Create a friendship safety spell by writing the name of a friend on a piece of paper and putting it in a bag with dried catnip. Speak the word *safety* as you tie the bag closed, and keep it in a safe place.

Describe your friend here. Write about what they mean to you.

I am manifesting inner strength.

Using red ink, create your own sigil for confidence.

Find inspiration from the confidence of nature around you.

Draw your sigil!

I let go of fear.

Create your first spell jar for confidence! Using one of your upcycled jars, place inside it catnip for Earth, carnelian for fire, full-moon water for water, and the smoke from a red candle for air. As you add each item, say, "Confidence," loudly into the jar, and then seal it.

Describe the most recent time you felt confident enough to tackle the whole world. What was so special about that moment?

My inner beauty shines through.

Add a little beauty magic to your day by incorporating something red—be it lipstick or your choice of clothing—into your look for a boost of confidence.

List five favorite items in your closet that make you feel confident. What do you love about them?

Witchcraft helps me find my strength.

With red ink, take some time to write about your journey with self-confidence. Write about areas you have grown to celebrate and areas you are still struggling to let go or accept.

_____

_____

_____

_____

_____

_____

_____

_____

_____

_____

_____

_____

_____

I am focused on my future.

Carnelian is amazing for focus. Place a carnelian at your workstation, and every time you find your mind wandering, look to your carnelian to harness the ability to get you through your task.

List three habits that you have been trying to break. Pick one of them to focus on, and make a list of small steps to accomplish it. Make sure these are small manageable goals!

_____

_____

_____

_____

_____

_____

_____

_____

_____

_____

I banish
stagnant energy
from my life.

If you are looking to banish stagnant energy from a room, a red candle is the fastest-acting one there is. Try it in a rarely used room or closet by lighting a red candle and blowing it out, letting the smoke carry away the lingering energies.

Every goal I set is achievable.

Press and dry a large catnip leaf to use as a bookmark in this journal for added courage in writing new spells.

Make a list of five ways you have shown courage in the last year. Use these to remind yourself that you are strong.

_____

_____

_____

_____

_____

_____

_____

_____

_____

_____

_____

_____

_____

I am allowed to just be.

Develop confidence in your ability to rest when you need it by taking naps throughout the week.

Write about your dreams here.

Fear is only a feeling; it cannot hold me back.

In the spirit of the confidence that you are manifesting, try something new this week, whether that be a new spell, activity, game, or restaurant!

Brainstorm five ways to approach life with a new attitude.

Magic brings me strength.

Using red ink, write about your inner warrior and how your inner warrior witch will help carry you through the rest of the year.

_____

_____

_____

_____

_____

_____

_____

_____

_____

_____

_____

_____

I am worthy of relaxation's embrace.

Make time to slow down and spend an evening reading by candle-light. Choose a candle that soothes you in smell, shape, or color. Remember that white candles are interchangeable for all colors.

Write about your sensory experience here.

_____

_____

_____

_____

_____

_____

_____

_____

_____

_____

_____

_____

_____

My dynamic energy attracts positivity.

Oranges and orange peel are used as the embodiment of the sun in spell work. They add their fiery energy to spells for happiness, positive energy, and wealth.

Write down any spells for happiness, positivity, and wealth here.

Small frustrations will not bother me today.

We can unintentionally hold in excess frustration. Light several orange candles, and blow them out one by one. Visualize the smoke carrying the frustrations away from your body.

What sensations do you notice in your body? Do you feel lighter?

My spells succeed.

Write down a few witchy tools you would like to study more deeply to help you keep track of your progress in self-education.

_____

_____

_____

_____

The universe is on my side.

Salt is a common tool used for purification and consecration rituals. Create your own blessed salt by holding a jar in your hands and asking that the good energies of the universe infuse it.

What are some areas of your life that you would like to imbue with more positivity or joy?

_____

_____

_____

_____

_____

_____

_____

_____

_____

_____

_____

_____

I am ready to welcome my highest good.

Research a farm near you that does self-pick produce, and plan a trip. Meditate on the differences between food collected with your own hands and food purchased at a grocery store.

I let go of beliefs that are limiting me.

On a full moon, sit under the rays and meditate on what beliefs you may have been holding on to that are keeping you from living a life full of joy. Allow the moon to wash them away one by one.

How did it feel to sit with your thoughts under the moon's rays? How do you incorporate mindfulness in your life?

I am open to receiving answers from the universe.

Oranges were historically used for divination. It is said that if you ask an orange a yes or no question and then count its seeds, you will have your answer. An odd number of seeds means no, and an even number of seeds means yes.

What questions are you asking, and how is the universe responding?

_____

_____

_____

_____

_____

_____

_____

_____

_____

_____

Magic runs through me.

Amber is often warm to the touch. Hold the amber in your hands, and think about its warmth spreading through your body.

Meditate on what areas seem to need the warmth the most and how you can support them.

I create the environment for my emotions.

Along with encouragement, orange candles can symbolize discipline. Light an orange candle at the same time every night for a week. Once complete, think about what you can do every night at the same time to encourage yourself for the next day.

Describe your nighttime routine here.

What I will becomes true.

					IDEAL TIME TO CAST	
INGREDIENTS	STONES	HERBS	CANDLES	SIGILS	OBJECTS	OTHER
WORDS						
INSTRUCTIONS						

Create your own spell with an orange or orange peel at the center of the working. What does the spell represent to you? What other ingredients have you chosen?

I can see the blessings around me.

Write a letter to a friend today to tell them the joy that they bring into your life. Seal it with orange wax to magically send your energy of happiness..

I create a plan of action.

Create a vision board for a long-term goal and use it as a visual aid in crafting the perfect spells and manifestations for you to achieve your goal.

Brainstorm your vision board here.

I begin each day with a joyful heart.

Pulling from all your joyful experiences with the
Earth recently, draw a sigil that symbolizes joy to you.
(Tip: You can make a destructible, temporary,
or permanent sigil here!)

I complete what
I set my mind to.

Clearing out old tasks is a form of self-care. Choose three small tasks that you can complete over the span of a week.

_____

_____

_____

_____

_____

_____

_____

_____

_____

_____

_____

_____

_____

The universe is there to support me.

Repetition helps with manifestation. Write out a plan of action to complete the tasks that you chose yesterday. What herbs and crystals can help support you while you complete them?

My mind is full of brilliant ideas.

Yellow candles are filled with bright energy, which makes them perfect for spell work involving intelligence, focus, or social skills.

Write down some spells or manifestations that could be enhanced by a yellow candle.

My manifestations are filled with strength.

Citrine is one of two crystals that never has to be cleansed, as it transmutes energies rather than absorbs them. This makes citrine the crystal of choice for spells related to manifestation, personal will, and generosity.

My thoughts are full of sweetness.

Chamomile's sweetness and beauty make it excellent for spell work for protection, purification, and relaxation. Plant chamomile near entrances to your home to add a protective barrier against negative energies, or add shredded chamomile leaves to a small sachet to carry with you when you feel you may need protection.

How can you use chamomile in your everyday life?

I understand that the things I desire take time to manifest.

					IDEAL TIME TO CAST	
INGREDIENTS	STONES	HERBS	CANDLES	SIGILS	OBJECTS	OTHER
WORDS						
INSTRUCTIONS						

Craft a four-week spell for long-term focus by carving four equi-distant lines horizontally on a yellow candle. Burn one section every Tuesday for four weeks while meditating on what you would like to direct your long-term focus toward.

I put good energy in the world, knowing I will receive it back.

Citrine is a crystal that promotes generosity. Embody this by gifting a citrine to a friend.

Write about the experience here.

_____

_____

_____

_____

_____

_____

_____

_____

_____

_____

_____

_____

My space is magical.

Every witch should have a space dedicated to their craft. Take some time to create an altar, or refresh yours if you already have one. This is your personal space to make magic and should represent you and your craft.

Use this space to plan your altar or brainstorm ways to enhance your existing one.

I release any negative energies I am holding on to.

For days when you are feeling vulnerable, create a spell bag to carry with you. Place citrine and dried chamomile in a yellow bag, and tie it closed with a red string. As you tie it, say, "I block negative energies from reaching me."

To continue the flow of positive energies, write down five affirmations to repeat to yourself as needed.

I am a creator filled with the sun's light.

To keep the sun with you at all times, craft a piece of art that represents the sun to keep in your home all year. Solar wheels, for example, are a simple craft using sticks and string or yarn. This is a terrific way to upcycle yarn from other craft projects.

What are some of your favorite things to do in the sun, and how can you do them more often?

_____

_____

_____

_____

_____

_____

_____

_____

_____

_____

Working with the elements brings me joy.

Blue candles represent both Earth and water, and are soothing additions to spell work for creativity, guidance, and peace.

What is something you believe in that helps guide you and shape your life?

_____

_____

_____

_____

_____

_____

_____

_____

_____

_____

_____

_____

The journey to wisdom is the journey through self-awareness.

Lapis lazuli has been known as the wisdom stone, which sets the tone for usefulness in spells for truth, self-awareness, and self-expression.

Write what things in your life already add to your self-expression and ways you can incorporate lapis lazuli (or your alternative) into that.

My wishes will be granted.

Write a wish (or three) on bay leaves and burn them in your cauldron (or fire-safe container). This releases your wish(es) to the universe with the powerful victory energy that bay leaves bring.

Write down some affirmations to reinforce your wishes and to keep them in mind.

My body is healthy.

Bay leaves are not only a powerful magical herb but also a delicious one. Incorporate them into a meal today, and physically take in the energy of peace they bring.

Write down a comfort-food recipe to make that could help you relax and unwind. (Bay leaves optional!)

Simple magics are beautiful.

Ringing a bell is a simple and beautiful way to clear a space before and after performing magic in it. Ring a bell now to clear your space. Alternatively, tap a spoon on a glass to create a similar effect.

What spaces do you enjoy spending time in? Is there anything you can do to make the spaces more comfortable for you?

I let go of the past.

Creating an environment of peace requires the releasing of unnecessary anger. Spray your altar with rose quartz spray to bring in self-love before lighting a blue candle. Visualize the flame burning away your anger.

What are some things you're still angry about? How can you work through that anger?

Magic brings me solace.

Create a sigil for peace, and place the sigil on your altar to bring the wish of peace to your life.

(Tip: You can also draw your sigil on a bay leaf for enhanced potency!)

Draw your sigil!

I am worthy of abundance.

Basil is an herb commonly found in kitchen gardens and is amazing for bringing abundance and success and dispelling confusion. Basil is easy to cultivate indoors with enough sun and water. Plant seeds or use a seedling to have basil on hand year-round.

What successes are you most proud of? What did you do to make them possible?

_____

_____

_____

_____

_____

_____

_____

_____

_____

_____

I bring the power of Earth to all that I do.

Brown candles represent double Earth power and bring their energies to spell work involving grounding, household resources, and fostering understanding. Collect and bless dirt or sand to add additional properties of Earth to your spells.

Write down the three things in your life that are most important to you right now. Why do they matter so much?

_____

_____

_____

_____

_____

_____

_____

_____

_____

_____

_____

I trust my intuition to guide me through life's questions.

Tiger's eye is amazing for balancing energies and grounding due to its combined representation of fire and Earth. It works well with spells involving clear thinking, developing skills, and manifestation.

What is something you've been trying to figure out lately? This could be a problem that needs a solution, or a question about one of life's mysteries.

I release
stagnant energies.

Cleansing our own bodies is just as important as cleansing our other tools. Wash your hands and perform a smoke cleanse with the incense or herb of your choice.

Sometimes, even the greatest goals are achieved through a series of small steps. What small steps can you celebrate today?

New environments bring me new energy.

Change things up! Take a new route to an old place and see how it enhances your perspective of your environment.

How did it feel? Did you notice anything new about your environment? How can you add an extra bit of mindfulness to each day?

I am in sync with the moon.

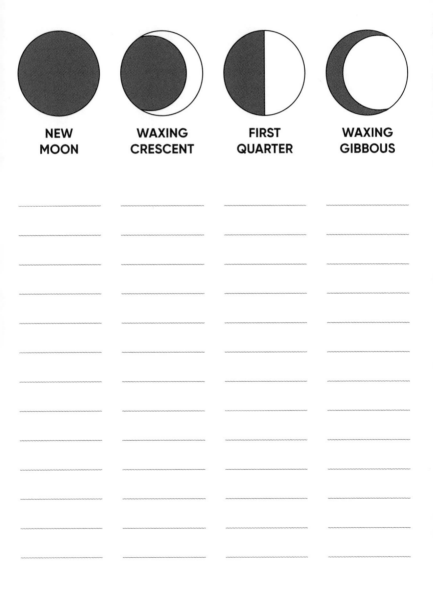

NEW MOON	WAXING CRESCENT	FIRST QUARTER	WAXING GIBBOUS

Write the dates of the moon phases. Be mindful of when each phase occurs. On full moons, you can recharge your crystals and supplies by letting them bathe in the moonlight.

FULL MOON	WANING GIBBOUS	THIRD QUARTER	WANING CRESCENT

I feel rooted and secure in my own space.

Write three things that make you feel grounded in your space. How can you incorporate them into your next spell for grounding?

Chaos has no place in my life.

Brown candles are excellent for eliminating chaos. Dress a brown candle with herbs for a future time of need.

What are three things that you do to feel more organized in your daily life?

_____

_____

_____

_____

_____

_____

_____

_____

_____

_____

_____

I will have all that I ask for.

Not all wishes want to be burned. Create a box where you can store your written wishes and manifestations while they grow to completion. Decorate it with crystals and symbols that bring power to your craft.

Describe five values that are essential to who you are. Why are these important to you? How can they help you see your wishes realized?

_____

_____

_____

_____

_____

_____

_____

_____

_____

Creating structure in my life aids in my ability to manifest my desires.

Fluorite is a crystal of structure. It aids in spell work for balance, allows you to embrace challenging emotions, and promotes impartiality.

Write down a piece of advice that changed your life. Is there anyone you know who could use this same advice right now?

I allow the universe to speak to me.

Take time today to meditate on different forms of divination that you may be interested in.

Summarize what you learn here.

I am full of possibility.

Divination is a practice that gives many witches an outlet to use their magic energies and receive messages from the universe. Choose a form of divination to study.

How can you use divination in your magical practice or daily life?

I am deeply connected to my magic.

Purple candles are said to reveal hidden knowledge, making them the perfect candles to use when performing spell work for creativity, dreams, and stress relief. Light a purple candle to aid in relief from stress and bring creativity into your magical work.

Describe a recent situation where you felt overwhelmed or like you couldn't handle things. Then write down what happened afterward. What did you do?

Knowing I create my own magic fills me with inner calm.

Lavender is best known for its ability to help us sleep, but it is also used in spell work for devotion, inner calm, and purification. Create a space to begin drying your own herbs to use in your magical work.

What herbs do you find that you use the most in your daily life? Are there others herbs you want to experiment with? List them here along with potential uses.

_____

_____

_____

_____

_____

_____

_____

_____

_____

_____

I nourish my mind as well as my body.

Tea

TYPE	AROMA	TASTE	THOUGHTS
Black			
Chamomile			
Earl Grey			
English Breakfast			
Lemon			
Mint			

Tea can have restorative and calming effects on the nervous system and can boost your immune system and help prevent certain diseases.

Try out different kinds of tea to see which ones you like. Write about the aroma, the taste, and any reflections you have about your preferences.

TYPE	AROMA	TASTE	THOUGHTS
Hibiscus			
Jasmine			
Ginger			

Things are crystallizing into place for me.

Fluorite is excellent at bridging the gap between mental and physical, which makes it amazing for organization. Place it in a room that needs a little extra organization, and let fluorite support you in making a plan of action.

Write your plan of action here.

_____

_____

_____

_____

_____

_____

_____

_____

_____

_____

I have the power to accomplish what I set my mind to.

A poppet is used in magical and spell work to represent yourself. Create a dream poppet by cutting two rough figures of a human out of purple cloth, sewing them almost completely together, and then stuffing it with lavender and other herbs that bring you a sense of calm and peace.

Put the poppet under your pillow one night, and write about any dreams you might have.

(Tip: Light a purple candle and spend time meditating before bed. Blow out the candle, and let the smoke infuse your dream poppet before putting it under your pillow.)

I am a visionary witch; my dreams shape my reality.

Create a peaceful sleep candle for future need. A whole plethora of options are available: carve it with sigils or words, anoint it with oil or honey, cover it in herbs, or embed crystals inside of it.

How have your dreams influenced your waking life?

I listen to myself with clarity and trust.

Bundle long stems of dried lavender with a purple ribbon to create a wand that embodies inner calm and spiritual enlightenment.

What are some ways you dismiss your own intuition or inner guidance? How can you listen to and engage with yourself more?

Caring for my magic is caring for myself.

Self-care is caring for your magic space. Infuse lavender in white vinegar, and use it to give your altar a quick freshening up while promoting a sense of serenity.

What recurring patterns do you notice in your life, and how do they impact you?

I am allowed to create new boundaries.

Black candles are primarily used for banishing spells. This aids in removing bad habits, dispelling negative energies, and creating a protective environment for spell craft. Light a black candle while focusing on protecting your energy.

Write about a time when you didn't stay true to your boundaries in a relationship. How did that make you feel?

_____

_____

_____

_____

_____

_____

_____

_____

_____

_____

I am protected by my magic.

Black salt is a powerful protection tool. Make black salt by grinding together whole black peppercorns and sea salt. Use this to add power to protection and banishing spells.

What are some techniques or strategies you find helpful for protecting yourself or managing stress?

_____

_____

_____

_____

_____

_____

_____

_____

_____

_____

_____

Through giving, I also receive.

Service to others is an important part of witchcraft. Find a place where you can lend a hand this month.

What did you learn from your experience? How can you apply what you have learned to your own life?

I am open to all messages the universe sends me.

Start a dream journal or dedicate a section of the notes section in the back of this journal to writing down your dreams. Messages come in every plane we inhabit.

I am transforming myself.

Is there a lingering habit you cannot seem to shake? Create a seven-day candle spell for yourself by carving seven equidistant lines horizontally into a large taper candle. Each line represents one day. Light this candle every day for one week, burning only to the next carved line.

Write down the spectrum of emotions you feel as each day progresses.

My mind and energy are calm.

Amethyst is a crystal known for calming the mind. It imparts courage, serenity, and wisdom to spell work.

How does your body physically respond when you are experiencing anxiety? How can you use crystals, herbs, tea, or other natural sources to help alleviate those feelings?

I forgive myself.

Hold an amethyst in your hands and imbue it with the power of serenity.

Carry it with you on occasions where you feel you need additional calm and comfort. Do you notice a difference?

The moon guides my magic.

Mugwort is described as "the lunar herb." It is highly regarded for its powers to aid divination work as well as its value as a protective herb. Add mugwort to your dream poppet to invite divinatory dreams to visit you.

Write about any dreams you had in your dream journal.

I allow everyday magic to fill my life.

Press a fresh mugwort leaf to act as a bookmark in a dream journal (if you have one!) or somewhere in this journal. Let its powers aid you in clearly remembering your dreams.

Déjà rêvé is the feeling of having already dreamed something you are experiencing. Do you have any experience with this concept?

_____

_____

_____

_____

_____

_____

_____

_____

_____

_____

_____

_____

I accept my shadow self.

Create a sigil for protection. This can be used in spells and even
embroidered on your clothes. Practice drawing it on the next page.

Draw your sigil!

I am prepared to use magic to aid myself.

Preparation is part of protection. Craft a protection candle by carving your sigil into it and adorning it with herbs and crystals you feel called to.

What is a ritual you can perform with the protection candle? What do you want to ask of the universe?

_____

_____

_____

_____

_____

_____

_____

_____

_____

_____

_____

I accept myself as whole.

Amethyst's powers are enhanced when worn against the skin.

Wear amethyst today and write about how it changed your day.

I know good things take time.

Create mugwort oil for anointing tools with divinatory or protection powers. Finely chop fresh or dried mugwort, and place it in a jar. Fully cover the herb in avocado oil and allow it to meld for up to six weeks. The longer it sits, the stronger it will be.

Write about a divinatory practice you want to explore that can be enhanced with the mugwort oil.

My path is filled with knowledge.

What did you learn from your study into divination? Is this a tool that speaks to you? Write about your journey here.

_____

_____

_____

_____

_____

_____

_____

_____

_____

_____

_____

_____

_____

_____

I am following my path.

Look back at the vision board you created earlier (or create a vision board if you haven't already)! What things have you achieved? What goals have changed?

Update or design your vision board with a particular focus on your own self-growth.

I can transform energies around me.

Engender a calm and balanced home by placing an amethyst in a room that sees a lot of activity.

Did you notice a change in the room? How else might you provide a sense of calm to an energetic room?

My senses are attuned.

Scrying is an ancient form of divination that uses reflective surfaces such as crystal balls and black mirrors. Make your own black mirror by taking the glass out of a frame and spray-painting the back of the glass with black paint. Allow it to dry, and place it back in the frame for a scrying tool made by your hands.

How might you use your scrying tool?

My hands create my protection.

Make a mugwort wreath to decorate your altar and add its powers of protection and prophecy to all your rituals.

Write down some manifestations regarding protection here for later inspiration.

_____

_____

_____

_____

_____

_____

_____

_____

_____

_____

_____

_____

Color fills my life
and my magic.

Silver candles are most often used in magic calling on the moon but are also useful in spells for divination, healing, and purification.

What are some rituals you might use a silver candle for?

I am grateful
for my community.

Write thank-you letters to people in your life. List the people you are sending letters to and write about what candle you think speaks to them. Seal the letters with wax from that candle.

How did it feel to handwrite letters to the people you feel gratitude toward?

I am strong enough to solve my problems.

Labradorite is known for aiding the development of new skills as well as its ability to strengthen will and empower transformation. Place a piece of labradorite or your alternative on your altar to help it aid your magical strength of will.

How have you changed in the past month? In the past year? In the past few years?

I bring the power of water to all that I do.

A chalice represents water on your altar and can be used for decoration or for ceremonial drinks. Buy, thrift, or upcycle a glass as a chalice for your altar. It can be as simple or as elaborate as you want it to be.

How might you incorporate the other elements into your altar?

_____

_____

_____

_____

_____

_____

_____

_____

_____

_____

_____

_____

I grow what I need to fulfill my life.

Sage is a common garden herb included in many recipes, and it is widely used in cleansing rituals. It carries the powers of good luck, prosperity, and wisdom. Sage is another herb that does well when cultivated indoors. Plant seeds or seedlings to add to your growing fresh herb collection.

How can you continue to add to your herb collection? What herbs would be helpful to you in this moment?

_____

_____

_____

_____

_____

_____

_____

_____

_____

_____

The universe grants my requests.

Request a boost to your powers of intuition by lighting a silver candle and making the request out loud. Allow the candle to burn out on its own.

Write down your request here as many times as you feel you need to add to its strength.

I release my attachment to the outcome.

Grind dried sage to add wisdom to any spell work. Store most of this sage for later work, but sprinkle a small amount on the crown of your head, and ask that the sage grant you the power of wisdom in your decisions.

Are you struggling with any decisions right now? Write a short pro and con list, reflecting on what choice might best serve you.

I have everything
I need within myself.

	STONES	HERBS	CANDLES	SIGILS	OBJECTS	OTHER
					IDEAL TIME TO CAST	
INGREDIENTS						
WORDS						
INSTRUCTIONS						

Silver is an amazing color for healing. Craft a healing spell centered on silver candles and incorporate lavender for calmness.

How do you handle tough emotions, thoughts, or memories? What helpful healing strategies do you employ?

I allow my magic to guide me to knowledge.

Use a piece of labradorite to unlock untapped creative powers. Place the crystal on the pages of this journal, and ask it to bring to mind creative endeavors you should try.

Write all the words that come to mind for the next two minutes on the paper, and watch the labradorite guide you in your new direction.

I am a magnet for calming energy.

Bundle dried sage and tie it with twine to create a smudge stick. Light the bundle, and then "smudge" it (extinguish the flame by gently rubbing it against a rock or the ground). After, bathe in the purifying smoke.

What experiences provide the most relaxation and relief for you? Write about them here.

_____

_____

_____

_____

_____

_____

_____

_____

_____

_____

_____

Success is drawn to me.

Place a sage leaf in your wallet to bring prosperity to your finances.

What is your definition of success? How have you been successful in your life so far?

My energy is sacred.

Create a sigil for purification. Using your finger, draw this sigil on items you would like to cleanse but cannot be touched by water.

Draw your sigil!

I am deeply fulfilled by what I do.

Dance like no one is watching. The power of movement can add energy to our spells and our everyday lives. Take time to dance in your favorite room of the house.

What are some positive things you can do every day to boost your mood?

_____

_____

_____

_____

_____

_____

_____

_____

_____

_____

_____

The power of the sun fills my life.

Gold candles represent the sun and are useful in spell work involving attraction, fame, and positivity. Create a special place to light a gold candle to bring positivity into any day. Add additional items that bring you joy or amplify your spell.

How would you describe your ideal day? Can you make it happen?

Balance is a part of my life.

Garnets are used to balance the physical with the spiritual and aid in spell work involving intimacy, success, and travel. Craft a simple balancing spell using garnet and an herb or crystal that evokes grounding for you. Place them together, and chant today's affirmation.

What are the causes of some of your unhealthy behavior patterns? How can you adjust or break them to achieve more balance in your life?

I can go with the flow.

Cinnamon is a heavily used herb in spell work due to its strength and versatile nature. It's useful in success spells, protection charms, and luck spells of all varieties. Cinnamon adds speediness to any spell. Add it to the next spell you need in a hurry, or sprinkle it on a letter you would like to arrive quickly and safely.

Describe a time where you showed just how strong you really are. How can you infuse that strength into your everyday life?

_____

_____

_____

_____

_____

_____

_____

_____

Success flows toward me.

Make a paired candle spell by placing a green candle right next to a gold candle. Light them at the same time, and ask that the candles aid each other in bringing success into your life.

What are five things you will never change about yourself?

My journey is filled with peace.

Traveling is always hard. Ease your next journey by making a travel amulet to carry with you. Place a garnet, mugwort, and lavender in a small bag with a long string. As you tie it closed, ask the universe to grant you smooth travels.

If you could spend one year in any country in the world, where would you go? Where else is on your travel bucket list?

_____

_____

_____

_____

_____

_____

_____

_____

_____

_____

I am in communication with the universe.

When have you felt déjà vu? Create a thought web of the event, and try to connect it with other memories or associations. What do you make of it?

I am surrounded by calm and protected from stress.

Create a protection charm for any doorway by putting blessed salt in a bag, tying it closed with white string, and attaching a stick of incense to it.

Write down five things that calm you down. Are there certain scents and sounds that help you de-stress?

I am a master of manifesting.

To make space for the universe to bring you more abundance, donate three items from your wardrobe that you no longer wear.

How do you define your style—that special something that makes you YOU?

I embody forgiveness.

Use cinnamon in a meal today to imbue your food with the powers of love and strength. Cinnamon is as versatile in food as it is in spell work and makes a great addition to sweet or savory dishes.

How do you measure happiness? Jot down your favorite things to do when you need a pick-me-up.

_____

_____

_____

_____

_____

_____

_____

_____

_____

_____

_____

_____

Everything I touch turns to gold.

Dress a gold candle with cinnamon to add strength to the power of the sun the candle holds. Use this candle to illuminate a room and bring the sun inside at a dark time of the year.

What ten things have made you laugh recently? Do you see any patterns?

Magic protects me.

Make a Yule log by purifying a log or stick, decorating it with pine, and adding three candles of your choice to represent the elements and the season. The most common candle choices are gold, green, red, silver, and white.

Write down what you need to create your Yule log and any inspiration!

(Tip: While Yule logs are often associated with the winter holidays, feel free to get creative here!)

I work with what nature gifts me.

Full of fiery energy, garnet adds its energy to spell work and other crystals it is stored with. Place your garnet with another crystal in your home, or add it to a spell in progress to amplify the power.

What are five things that bring purpose to your life? Describe and reflect on how they have impacted who you are today.

_____

_____

_____

_____

_____

_____

_____

_____

_____

_____

Good health is drawn to me.

Fill your night with light. Light candles in every room of your house and bask in the glow and warmth they provide. Try grouping different candles together, and see if it changes the energy of the room.

In what type of environment do you feel the most energized? What place are you in? What people are there, or are you by yourself?

Every action
I take is magical.

Silence and stillness create their own magic. Take five minutes to sit
in silence, and allow your magic to flow through stillness.

Do you find comfort in silence? What kind of thoughts or sensations come to mind?

I release my mistakes and embrace my future.

Write a list of magical goals for the new year (or the current year!) See where you can use your magical knowledge to choose the perfect timing for them.

_____

_____

_____

_____

_____

_____

_____

_____

_____

_____

_____

_____

_____

_____

_____

I have the power to transform the environment around me.

Find something old in your house and make it new. This can be a piece of clothing, a jar, or a pantry item.

What was the object in the past, and what is it going to be in the future?

I see through
to my true aura.

Color this spread with a shade that you

feel best represents your aura.

I remain connected to my happiness.

Write down things that never fail to make you happy or bring a smile to your face. Return to this list when you are feeling down

_____

_____

_____

_____

_____

_____

_____

_____

_____

_____

_____

_____

_____

I create magic in all that I do.

Write down all the things you have accomplished this year. Revitalize your magic with self-appreciation.

Throw yourself a party! You have taken yourself through an entire journal of everyday witchcraft, and that deserves celebration.

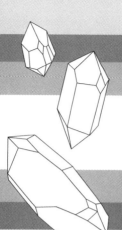

My Spells

Write all your spells in the last pages of this journal. Keep adding to them as you continue your journey.

Spell suggestions:

Attracting Love	Fertility	Persuasion
Binding	Grounding	Protection
Blessings	Healing	Rain
Cleansing	Luck	Safe Travels
Divinations	Memory	Sleeping

		IDEAL TIME TO CAST

	STONES	HERBS	CANDLES	SIGILS	OBJECTS	OTHER
INGREDIENTS						

WORDS

INSTRUCTIONS

Spell Record

DATE	TIME	SEASON	MOON	RESULT
			○	
			○	
			○	
			○	
			○	
			○	
			○	
			○	
			○	

			IDEAL TIME TO CAST

	STONES	HERBS	CANDLES	SIGILS	OBJECTS	OTHER
INGREDIENTS						

WORDS	

INSTRUCTIONS	

Spell Record

DATE	TIME	SEASON	MOON	RESULT
			◯	
			◯	
			◯	
			◯	
			◯	
			◯	
			◯	
			◯	
			◯	

	IDEAL TIME TO CAST

	STONES	HERBS	CANDLES	SIGILS	OBJECTS	OTHER
INGREDIENTS						

WORDS

INSTRUCTIONS

Spell Record

DATE	TIME	SEASON	MOON	RESULT
			◯	
			◯	
			◯	
			◯	
			◯	
			◯	
			◯	
			◯	
			◯	

				IDEAL TIME TO CAST

	STONES	HERBS	CANDLES	SIGILS	OBJECTS	OTHER
INGREDIENTS						

WORDS

INSTRUCTIONS

Spell Record

DATE	TIME	SEASON	MOON	RESULT
			◯	
			◯	
			◯	
			◯	
			◯	
			◯	
			◯	
			◯	
			◯	

	IDEAL TIME TO CAST

	STONES	HERBS	CANDLES	SIGILS	OBJECTS	OTHER
INGREDIENTS						

WORDS	

INSTRUCTIONS	

Spell Record

DATE	TIME	SEASON	MOON	RESULT

				IDEAL TIME TO CAST

	STONES	HERBS	CANDLES	SIGILS	OBJECTS	OTHER
INGREDIENTS						

WORDS	

INSTRUCTIONS	

Spell Record

DATE	TIME	SEASON	MOON	RESULT
			○	
			○	
			○	
			○	
			○	
			○	
			○	
			○	
			○	

	IDEAL TIME TO CAST

	STONES	HERBS	CANDLES	SIGILS	OBJECTS	OTHER
INGREDIENTS						

WORDS

INSTRUCTIONS

Spell Record

DATE	TIME	SEASON	MOON	RESULT
			◯	
			◯	
			◯	
			◯	
			◯	
			◯	
			◯	
			◯	
			◯	

	IDEAL TIME TO CAST

	STONES	HERBS	CANDLES	SIGILS	OBJECTS	OTHER
INGREDIENTS						

WORDS	

INSTRUCTIONS	

Spell Record

DATE	TIME	SEASON	MOON	RESULT
			◯	
			◯	
			◯	
			◯	
			◯	
			◯	
			◯	
			◯	
			◯	

	IDEAL TIME TO CAST

	STONES	HERBS	CANDLES	SIGILS	OBJECTS	OTHER
INGREDIENTS						
WORDS						
INSTRUCTIONS						

Spell Record

DATE	TIME	SEASON	MOON	RESULT
			○	
			○	
			○	
			○	
			○	
			○	
			○	
			○	
			○	

	IDEAL TIME TO CAST

	STONES	HERBS	CANDLES	SIGILS	OBJECTS	OTHER
INGREDIENTS						

WORDS	

INSTRUCTIONS	

Spell Record

DATE	TIME	SEASON	MOON	RESULT
			◯	
			◯	
			◯	
			◯	
			◯	
			◯	
			◯	
			◯	
			◯	

	IDEAL TIME TO CAST

	STONES	HERBS	CANDLES	SIGILS	OBJECTS	OTHER
INGREDIENTS						
WORDS						
INSTRUCTIONS						

Spell Record

DATE	TIME	SEASON	MOON	RESULT

					IDEAL TIME TO CAST

	STONES	HERBS	CANDLES	SIGILS	OBJECTS	OTHER
INGREDIENTS						

WORDS	

INSTRUCTIONS	

Spell Record

DATE	TIME	SEASON	MOON	RESULT
			◯	
			◯	
			◯	
			◯	
			◯	
			◯	
			◯	
			◯	
			◯	

	IDEAL TIME TO CAST

	STONES	HERBS	CANDLES	SIGILS	OBJECTS	OTHER
INGREDIENTS						

WORDS	

INSTRUCTIONS	

Spell Record

DATE	TIME	SEASON	MOON	RESULT
			○	
			○	
			○	
			○	
			○	
			○	
			○	
			○	
			○	

			IDEAL TIME TO CAST

	STONES	HERBS	CANDLES	SIGILS	OBJECTS	OTHER
INGREDIENTS						

WORDS	

INSTRUCTIONS	